Living in Neighborhoods

The Laidlaw Social Studies Series   **Skills and Concepts for Responsible Citizenship**

Beverly Jeanne Armento   **Jesus Garcia**   **Roy Erickson**

Herbert C. Rudman

Katherine T. Croft   **Barbara Foney**   **Francie D. Johnson**   **Marilyn Walker**

LAIDLAW BROTHERS · PUBLISHERS

A Division of Doubleday & Company, Inc.

RIVER FOREST, ILLINOIS

Irvine, California   Chamblee, Georgia   Dallas, Texas   Toronto, Canada

The Laidlaw Social Studies Series   Skills and Concepts for Responsible Citizenship

Living With People   Living in Families

Living in Neighborhoods   Living in Communities   Living in World Regions

Living in Our Country   Living in the World

Acknowledgments

Project Director Wayne H. Talley / *Editor* Mary C. Ouska / *Production Director*
LaVergne G. Niequist / *Production Supervisor* Kathleen Kasper / *Photo Researcher*
William A. Cassin / *Art Director* Gloria J. Muczynski / *Designer* Dennis Horan /
Staff Technical Artist Susan Mills / *Artists* Frank Larocco; Susan Paradis;
John Walter and Associates: Joanna Adamska-Koperska and Jack Wallen

Photo Credits

Picture Group / Bohdan Hrynewych; Joseph A. DiChello Jr., cover, pages 1, 3, 4, 5.
Action-35 Photography/Don Lansu, 98, 99, 115 (left), 122. Alpha/Dave Bartruff, 176 (bottom). Alpha/Louis Goldman, 155. Alpha/J. Messerschmidt, 144–145, 178. Artstreet, 69, 71 (left), 72 (bottom), 124 (left), 131, 150 (left). Lee Balgemann, 92. Berg & Associates/Margaret C. Berg, 130 (top). Fredrik D. Bodin, 55, 115 (right). Daniel Brody, 94 (right). Cameramasters, 26, 91 (right). Camerique, 6–7, 9 (left), 20, 102, 116 (bottom left), 125 (top). Frank A. Cezus, 86. Chicago Historical Society/Mildred Mead, 138. Click/Chicago Ltd./ Donald Smetzer, 154 (right), 156 (right). Paul Conklin, 11 (top). Jack Corn, 34. Betty Crowell, 128 (right), 129 (both), 171 (right). John D. Cunningham, 112 (top). Dr. E.R. Degginger, 74 (bottom), 125 (bottom). Dr. E.R. Degginger/Frank Markowitz, Jr., 66. Leo de Wys Inc./Leonard Harris, 54. Leo de Wys Inc./Cliff Hausner, 133. Leo de Wys Inc./ Everett C. Johnson, 36, 61 (right), 126. Joseph A. Di Chello, Jr., 127. John D. Firestone, 101. FPG/Stephen Kotz, 176 (top). FPG/S. Younger, 154 (left). Grant Heilman, 8, 9 (right), 10, 35 (bottom), 110–111, 120, 142. Grant Heilman/Alan Pitcairn, 137 (right). Imagery, 60. Thomas Ives, 119, 148, 150 (right). Andrea Jacobsen, 94 (left), 104, 105, 106, 113 (bottom), 114, 117, 139. Brent Jones, 17 (left), 41 (left), 42 (bottom), 61 (left), 62, 76, 82 (left), 83 (bottom), 121, 130 (bottom). Lou Jones, 12 (right). Breck Kent, 25 (right). Joan Kramer and Associates, 58 (left), 112 (bottom). Tom McGuire, 72 (top). Christopher Mankus, 103 (right). Bill Means, 56, 89, 95. Durango Mendoza, 16 (left). Mary E. Messenger, 90 (top). Norma Morrison, 14 (top), 83 (top), 87, 88, 103 (left), 177. Odyssey Productions/Robert Frerck, 158 (both), 159, 160, 161 (both), 164, 165, 166. Chuck Pefley, 11 (bottom). Connie and P.C. Peri, 13 (both), 14 (bottom), 15, 22–23, 35 (top), 40, 41 (right), 50, 52–53, 57, 65, 68 (left), 73, 75, 78, 80–81, 96, 97, 100, 108. Chip and Rosa Maria Peterson, 149, 174. Photo Genesis/Ray Young, 132. Photo Network/James Stephens, 84. Photo Researchers/Bjorn Bolstad, 147. Photo Researchers/A. Louis Goldman, 153. Photo Researchers/Larousse, 156 (left). Photo Researchers/Michael Philip Manheim, 152 (both). Photo Trends/Victoria Beller-Smith, 17 (right), 65, 116 (right). Photo Trends/Thomas Chitty, 175. Photo Trends/Gloria Kaplan, 58 (right). Photo Trends/ Russell Thompson, 137 (left). Photri, 12 (left), 24, 31 (inset), 42 (top), 63. James H. Pickerell, 16 (top right), 18, 70, 113 (top), 116 (top left). Picture Group/Doug Bruce, 135. Picture Group/Anna Flynn, 134 (bottom). Picture Group/Jim Merrithew, 25 (bottom left). R/C Photo Agency/Richard L. Capps, 128 (left). G.R. Roberts, 168, 170. James P. Rowan, 25 (top left). Evelin Sanders, 85. Taurus/Laimute Druskis, 16 (bottom right). Taurus/Vance Henry, 169, 171 (left). Taurus/Eric Kroll, 59. Taurus/L.L.T. Rhodes, 74 (top). Taurus/Frank Siteman, 68 (right). Taurus/Summer Productions, 93. Jeanne Thompson Photography/Dr. Syd Radinovsky, 163. Mary Elenz Tranter, 90 (bottom), 91 (left), 118. University of Illinois Library at Chicago Circle Campus, 77 (right). Visualworld/Michele Burgess, 124 (right), 134 (top). Visualworld/Peter Keegan, 71 (right). Wide World, 77 (left).

ISBN 0–8445–6302–1

CONTENTS

LIST OF MAPS

LIST OF CHARTS

LIST OF GRAPHS

LIST OF UNIT-END SKILLS: BUILDING YOUR SKILLS

UNIT 1
WHAT IS A
NEIGHBORHOOD?

People live in different places.
Look at the picture.
What do you see in this picture?
How is this place like the place where you
    live?
How is it different?

1 WHAT NEIGHBORHOODS ARE

Communities are places where people live
   and share things.
Communities have many **neighborhoods.**
Neighborhoods are parts of communities.

People in a neighborhood live near one
    another.
They share special places.
Neighborhoods may have places to shop.
They may have places to learn.

Some neighborhoods have places of **worship.**
Worship is a way that people honor what
    they believe in.
Some neighborhoods have places to
    have fun.

CHECKING   What is a neighborhood?

MAIN

IDEAS

2 WHO LIVES IN NEIGHBORHOODS?

People who live in neighborhoods are
  neighbors.
Neighbors are the same in many ways.
Some neighbors care about the same things.
Some neighbors like to do the same things.

Neighbors are different, too.
They are different ages.
Neighbors belong to different families.

CHECKING MAIN IDEAS

1. What are some ways in which neighbors are the same?

2. What are some ways in which neighbors are different?

3 WHAT PEOPLE IN NEIGHBORHOODS DO

People in neighborhoods do many things.
Some people work.
Children go to school.
Some people worship.

People sometimes have fun together.
Some people help their neighbors.
Neighbors sometimes work together.
They help keep their neighborhood clean
    and safe.

Neighbors talk about the problems in their
neighborhood.
They do things to make their neighborhood
better.

CHECKING   What do people in neighborhoods do?

MAIN

IDEAS

4 WHY PEOPLE LIVE IN NEIGHBORHOODS

People live in neighborhoods to fill their
needs.
Needs are things people must fill in order to
live.
Food, clothes, and housing are needs.

People live in neighborhoods to fill their
  wants.
Wants are things people wish to have.
But they can live without these things.
Pets, games, and toys are wants.

People can fill some needs and wants in
their own neighborhood.
They fill other needs and wants in other
neighborhoods.

CHECKING
MAIN
IDEAS

1. Why do people live in neighborhoods?
2. What are some needs? Some wants?

Practicing Your Skills

Reading for Specific Information

You read for different things.
Sometimes you read to find answers.
Read to find out who neighbors are.

People who live in neighborhoods are
    neighbors.

The answer is <u>people who live in
    neighborhoods.</u>
Now read to find out how neighbors are
    the same.

Neighbors are the same in many ways.
Some neighbors care about the same
    things.

INVESTIGATING THE UNIT

Write your answers on a separate sheet of paper.

Using Words and Terms

Use the following words or terms in a sentence to show that you understand their meaning:

communities   neighborhoods
needs   wants
neighbors

Understanding Ideas

1. What is a neighborhood?
2. How are neighbors the same? How are they different?
3. What do neighbors do?
4. Where do people living in neighborhoods fill their needs and wants?

Building Your Skills

Read the stories below and answer the questions.

In Sue's neighborhood there are 49 places to live.

There are 2 food stores, 1 drugstore, and 4 places to have fun.

In Jack's neighborhood there are 53 places to live.

There is 1 food store and 2 places to have fun.

1. Whose neighborhood has more places to live?

2. Whose neighborhood has fewer places to have fun?

Making Decisions

Some people live in the same neighborhood all their life.

When you grow up, what kind of neighborhood would you like to live in? Why?

UNIT 2
WHERE ARE NEIGHBORHOODS?

Neighborhoods are in many different places.
These children want to find out where
    neighborhoods are.
What are these children looking at?
When have you used this same thing?

1 LOOKING AT THE EARTH

This is a picture of where we live.
We live on the earth.
This picture shows the earth from far away.

All parts of the earth do not look the same.
Some parts of the earth have land.
Other parts have water.

CHECKING Where do we live?

MAIN

IDEAS

2 LOOKING AT A GLOBE

This is a picture of a **globe.**
A globe is a model of the earth.
A globe shows what the earth looks like.
It shows land and water.

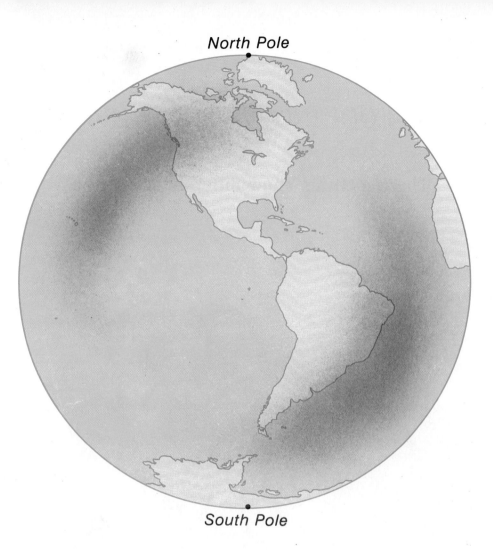

North Pole

South Pole

This is a picture of part of a globe.
Find the North Pole and the South Pole.

CHECKING
MAIN
IDEAS

1. What is a globe?
2. What are some things a globe shows?

3 LOOKING AT THE WORLD

These pictures show different parts of a
globe.

A globe shows **continents**.
Continents are large bodies of land.
A globe shows **oceans**.
Oceans are large bodies of water.

This is a **map.**

A map is a drawing of the earth.

A map shows all or part of the earth.

A world map shows all the earth.

It shows continents and oceans.

Find the continents and the oceans.

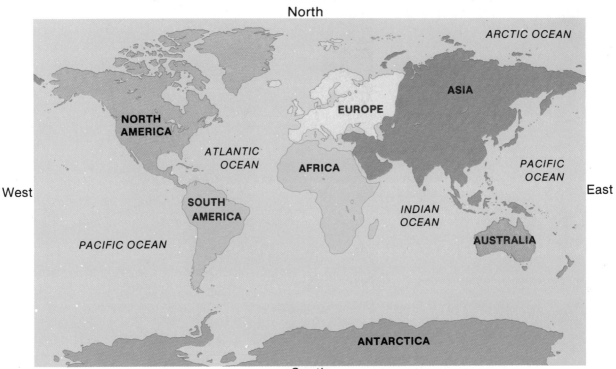

CHECKING MAIN IDEAS

1. What are continents?
2. What are oceans?
3. What is a map?

A Nation's Heritage

Meriwether Lewis and William Clark

Long ago, people didn't know much about
some parts of our country.
Meriwether Lewis and William Clark were
sent on a long trip.
They were asked to find out about our
country.
They made many maps that helped people
learn about a part of our country.

4 LOOKING AT THE UNITED STATES

This map shows the United States.
The United States is the country we live in.
The United States is made up of many parts
　　called states.

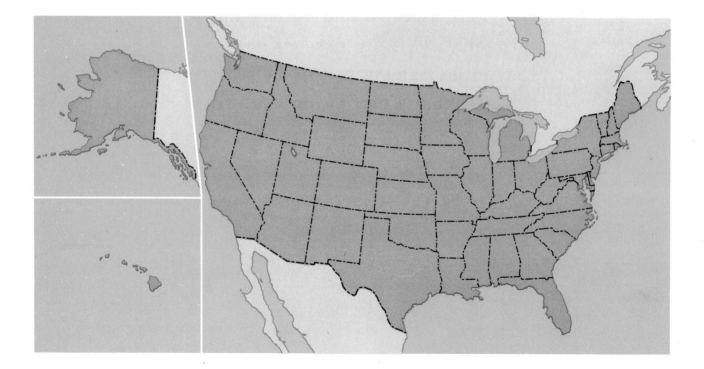

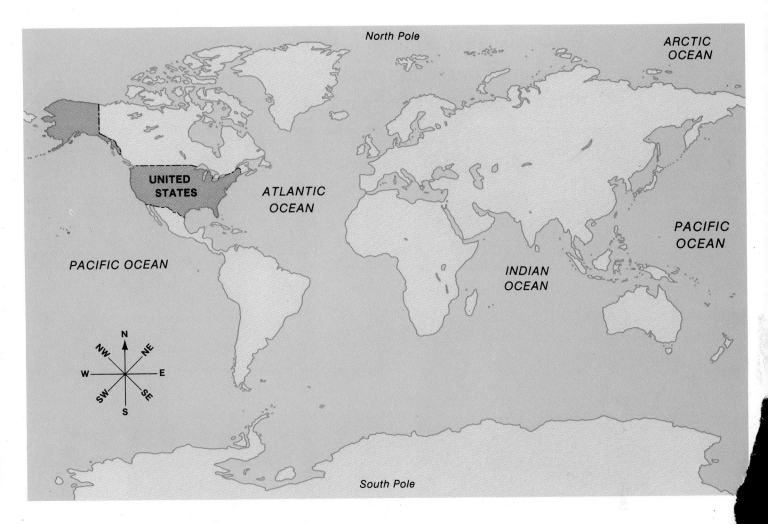

Find the United States on the map.
This map has a **compass rose.**
A compass rose shows directions.
Which way is north?

There are many communities in the United States.

These communities have neighborhoods like the ones in the pictures.

Which neighborhood is most like yours?

1

2

3

CHECKING What country do we live in?

MAIN

IDEAS

5 LOOKING AT WHERE WE ARE

This is a picture of a neighborhood.
What can you learn from this picture?
The map on page 37 is of the same
   neighborhood.
How is the map like the picture?

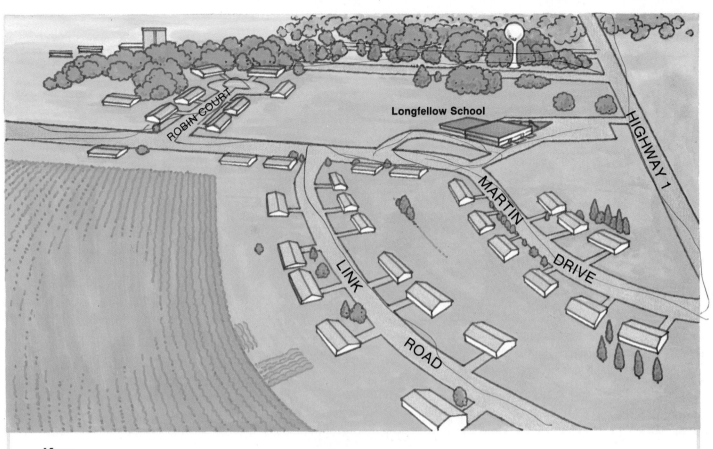

Key

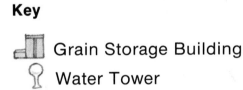 Grain Storage Building

 School

House

Water Tower

Playground

A map uses **symbols** to show houses, schools,
and other places.

A symbol is something that stands for
something else.

This map has a **map key.**

A map key tells what each symbol stands for.

Look at the map of Marco's neighborhood
   on page 39.
Marco starts at his house.
He goes north on First Street.
He goes past the firehouse.
Marco turns right on Maple Street.
He stops at the corner of Maple Street and
   Third Street.
Where is Marco going?

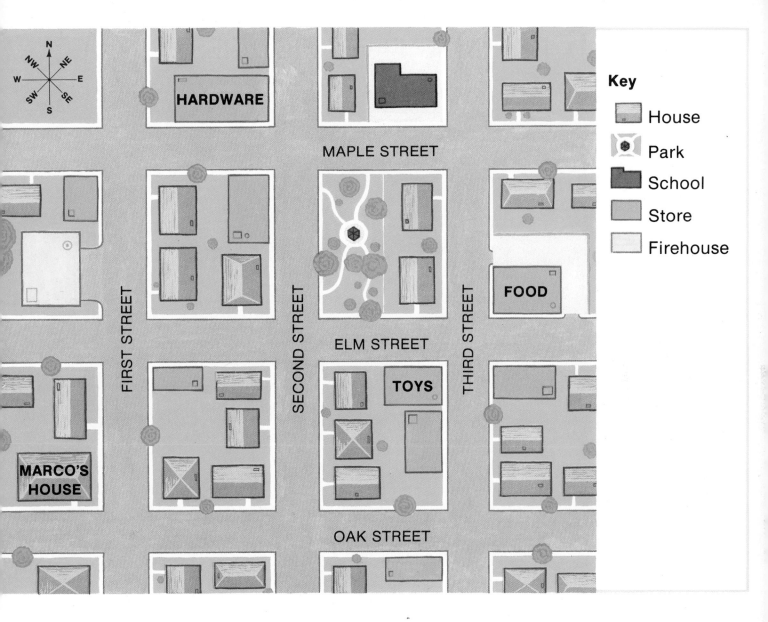

CHECKING What is a symbol?

MAIN

IDEAS

6 LEARNING FROM PICTURES

Pictures can help you learn about
  neighborhoods.
This is a picture of part of a neighborhood.
What can you learn about this
  neighborhood?

Pictures can help you learn about the places
in a neighborhood.
They can also help you learn about the
people.

Pictures can help you learn what people do.
What can you learn about the people in the
pictures on this page?

CHECKING
MAIN
IDEAS

What can you learn about neighborhoods
from pictures?

7 LEARNING FROM CHARTS

This is a **chart.**
It shows facts in a way that is easy to read.
What facts does this chart show?

Places in Neighborhoods

Kinds of Places	Martha's Neighborhood	John's Neighborhood	Roseanna's Neighborhood	Julio's Neighborhood
Places to Live	10	15	14	12
Places to Shop	6	7	3	5
Places to Learn	0	2	1	3
Places to Have Fun	1	3	0	2

Look at these neighborhood maps.
Make a chart.
Show the number of kinds of places in each
neighborhood.

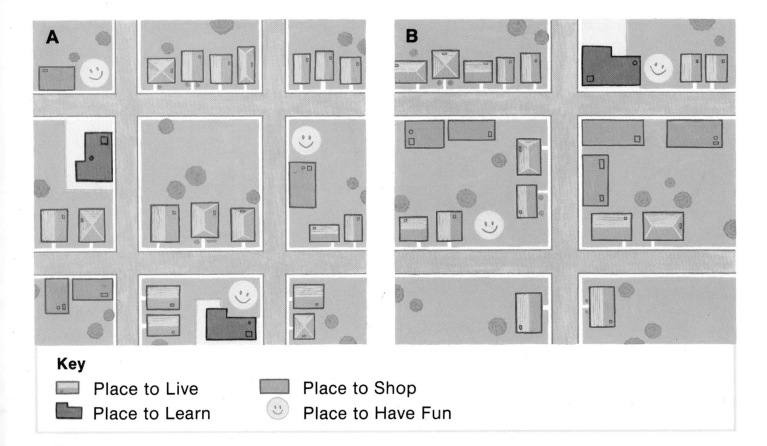

Key

▭ Place to Live   ▭ Place to Shop

▭ Place to Learn   ☺ Place to Have Fun

CHECKING   What does a chart show?

MAIN

IDEAS

Practicing Your Skills

Alphabetical Order

Look at the following words:
  chart
  globe
  model
  symbols

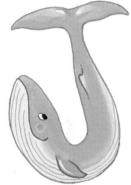

They are in **alphabetical order.**

The first letters of these words follow the
  order of the alphabet.

Put the following words in alphabetical
  order:

ocean	world
map	picture
continent	

8 LEARNING FROM DRAWINGS

Number of Places to Shop

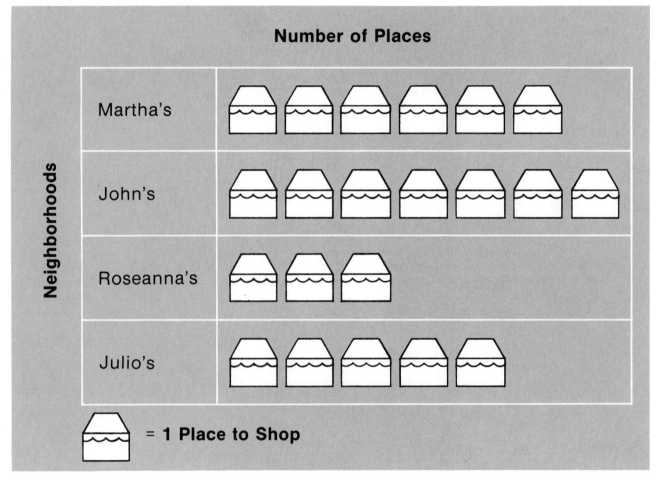

This drawing is a **pictograph.**
It uses pictures to show numbers of things.
What does each picture on this pictograph
   stand for?

Number of Places to Shop

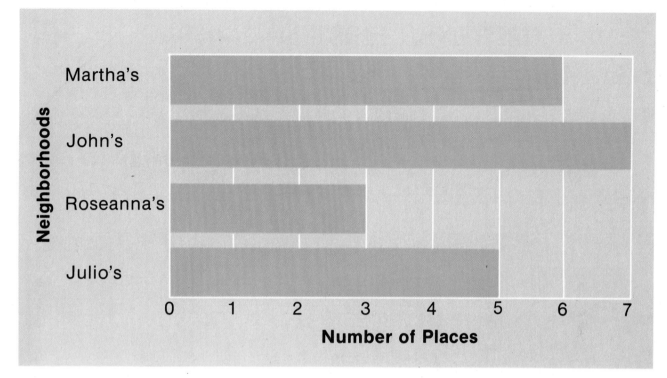

This is a **bar graph.**
Each bar shows numbers of things.
What does this bar graph show?
Pictographs and bar graphs are used to
   compare numbers of things.

CHECKING
MAIN
IDEAS

1. What is a pictograph?
2. What is a bar graph?

9 LEARNING WHICH HAPPENED FIRST

A

Pictures can help you learn the order in
  which things happened.
These are pictures of the same
  neighborhood.
They show the neighborhood at different
  times.
They tell a story about the neighborhood.
Put these pictures in order.
Which picture shows the neighborhood many
  years ago? A few years ago? Today?

B

C

CHECKING MAIN IDEAS

What can help you learn the order in which things happened?

INVESTIGATING THE UNIT

Write your answers on a separate sheet of paper.

Using Words and Terms

Use the following words or terms in a sentence to show that you understand their meaning:

globe	continents	oceans
map	compass rose	symbols
chart	pictograph	bar graph

Understanding Ideas

1. What are some things globes show?

2. What are some things maps show?

3. What does a chart show?

4. What do pictographs and bar graphs show?

Building Your Skills

Look at the map to the right. Answer the questions about the map.

1. What kinds of places are east of the clothing store?

2. In what direction is the food store from the toy store?

3. What kind of place is north of the place to learn?

Making Decisions

Tell if you could use a globe or a map to do the following things. If you could use either a globe or a map, say *both*.

1. Find out the shape of the earth

2. Find the continents and the oceans

3. Find places to shop in a neighborhood

4. Find the country we live in

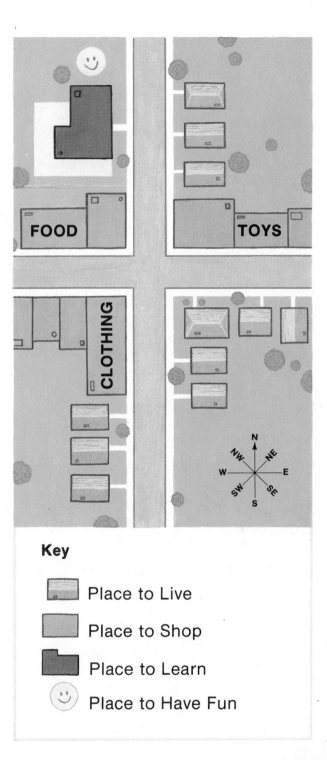

FOOD

TOYS

CLOTHING

Key

Place to Live

Place to Shop

Place to Learn

Place to Have Fun

UNIT 3
LEARNING ABOUT NEIGHBORHOODS

Neighborhoods have many kinds of places.
What kind of place is shown in this picture?
When have you gone to a place like this?
Does your neighborhood have a place like
this?

53

1 PLACES WHERE PEOPLE LIVE

Many people want to live near places to work, to shop, or to learn.
People live near these places to help fill some of their needs and wants.

People live in many different kinds of
  homes.
Some people live in houses.
Other people live in **mobile homes.**
Mobile homes are small houses that can be
  moved.

Many families live in an **apartment** building.
An apartment is a room or a group of rooms
   to live in.
What kind of home do you live in?

CHECKING   Why do people live where they do?

MAIN

IDEAS

2 PLACES WHERE PEOPLE MAKE THINGS

This picture shows people using **goods.**
Goods are things that help fill needs and
    wants.
Food, clothes, and toys are goods.

Goods such as shoes are usually made in
factories.
Factories are places where machines are
often used to make goods.
Some goods are made in small shops.
Some goods are made at home.

People often work together to make goods.
How are the people in this picture working
together?

CHECKING
MAIN
IDEAS

1. What are goods?
2. What are some places where goods are made?

3 PLACES WHERE PEOPLE DO THINGS FOR OTHERS

People cannot fill all their needs and wants
  by themselves.
Other people help them fill needs and wants.
Some people help others by making goods.

People also help others by providing
services.
Services are jobs that people do for others.
Doctors, teachers, and the police are a few of
the people who provide services.

People who provide services work in many different places.

Salespeople work in stores.

People who cut hair work in small shops.

Some carpet cleaners work in homes.

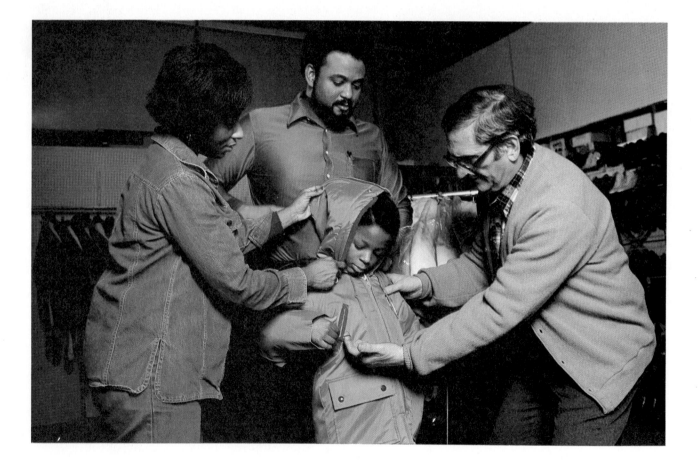

Fire fighters work where they are needed.
What are some other places where people
provide services?

CHECKING

MAIN

IDEAS

1. What are services?

2. What are some places where services are provided?

Practicing Your Skills

Using the Glossary

This is part of the **Glossary** of this book.

mobile homes

neighbors

A glossary tells what some words in a book mean.
Sometimes a glossary uses pictures to explain what the words mean.
A glossary is written in alphabetical order.

Find these words in the glossary.

| apartments | goods |
| factories | services |

4 PLACES WHERE PEOPLE SHOP

People buy goods and services at stores and
  shops.
Stores usually have many goods for sale.
A food store helps people fill their need for
  food.

Shops are usually small places where one
kind of good or service is sold.
A toy shop helps people fill their want for
toys.

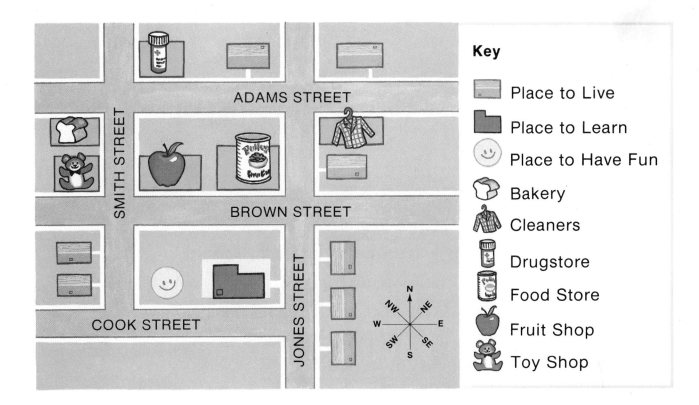

Answer these questions about places in
Inga's neighborhood.

What picture stands for the fruit shop?

What shop is north of the toy shop?

In what direction is the fruit shop from the
food store?

CHECKING
MAIN
IDEAS

Where do people buy some of the goods
and services they need or want?

5 PLACES WHERE PEOPLE LEARN

People can learn in different places.
Children can learn many things in school,
   such as how to read.
Other people can also learn things in school.
They might learn how to dance.

Some neighborhoods have a library.

People go to a library to read and to borrow books.

Some neighborhoods have a museum.

People might go to a museum to learn about the past.

Some neighborhoods have a neighborhood
    center.
People go to a neighborhood center to learn
    things with their neighbors.

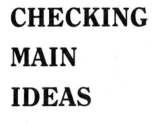

**CHECKING
MAIN
IDEAS**

What are some places where people can
learn?

6 PLACES WHERE PEOPLE WORSHIP

People have many different beliefs.

They worship in many different places.

As you have learned, worship is a way that
 people honor what they believe in.

Sometimes people worship in special places.

Sometimes people worship at home.

Some places of worship have special services.

Services might be quiet.

Services might have music.

Sometimes services help people remember
    special holidays.

CHECKING   What are some places where people
MAIN   sometimes worship?

IDEAS

7 PLACES WHERE PEOPLE HAVE FUN

Many neighborhoods have places where
   people can have fun.
Some neighborhoods have a playground.
A playground usually has special things to
   play on.

Some neighborhoods have a park.
People go to a park for picnics or to play.
Some parks have paths for people to walk.
Many parks have a pond where people
go fishing or boating.

74

Some neighborhoods have a theater.
People can see a play or a movie in a
theater.

Some neighborhoods have a place where
people can skate.
Some neighborhoods have a place to swim.

Some neighborhoods have an empty field
where children can play.
What places to have fun are in your
neighborhood?

CHECKING What are some places to have fun?

MAIN

IDEAS

A Nation's Heritage

Hull House

Hull House was the first neighborhood
　center in Chicago.
It was started by Jane Addams in 1889.
There were classes to teach people how to
　speak English.
There were meals for the hungry.
People who needed jobs were helped.
Today other neighborhood centers help
　people just as Hull House did long ago.

INVESTIGATING THE UNIT

Write your answers on a separate sheet of paper.

Using Words and Terms

Use the following words or terms in a sentence to show that you understand their meaning:

mobile homes   apartment

goods   services

Understanding Ideas

1. Why do many people live where they do?

2. What are some places where goods are made?

3. What are some places where services are provided?

4. What are some places where people can learn, worship, or have fun?

Building Your Skills

Use the following information to make a pictograph like the one to the right:

Lee's neighborhood has five houses.

It has a food store, a drugstore, a shoe store, a clothing store, and a gas station.

It also has a school, a library, a park, a theater, and a playground.

Making Decisions

Make believe that you and some of your friends went to a park for a picnic.

Just as you finished eating, a strong wind blew away some papers from your lunch.

What would you do or say if your friends said, "Let the papers blow away. Someone else will pick them up"?

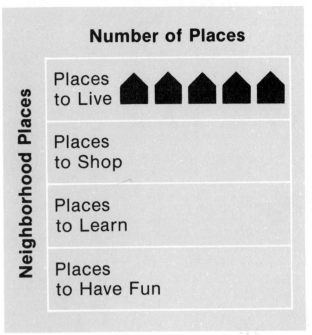

Places in Lee's Neighborhood

Number of Places

Neighborhood Places

Places to Live	▲ ▲ ▲ ▲ ▲
Places to Shop	
Places to Learn	
Places to Have Fun	

79

UNIT 4
WORKING TOGETHER IN GROUPS AND NEIGHBORHOODS

People want their neighborhood to be the best it can be.

Neighbors work together to try to do this.

Look at the picture.

How are these people working together?

81

1 BEING FRIENDLY

Neighbors show friendship by helping one
    another.
Sometimes they help one another when a
    job is too big to do alone.
Sometimes they help one another when
    someone is in trouble.

Neighbors show friendship by sharing.
They share neighborhood places.
They share neighborhood services.
Sometimes neighbors share things they own.

Neighbors show friendship by having fun
  together.
Sometimes they have picnics or parties with
  one another.
Sometimes neighbors play games together.

CHECKING   What are some ways in which neighbors

MAIN   show friendship?

IDEAS

2 GROUPS TO WHICH WE BELONG

You belong to many groups.
Your family is a group.
Your class in school is a group.
The children you play with are also a group.
What other groups do you belong to?

People belong to some groups to do special
things.
People belong to some groups to share
things with others.
People often belong to groups to work with
others.

CHECKING   Why do people belong to some groups?

MAIN

IDEAS

3 ROLES WITHIN GROUPS

People have a number of **roles.**
Roles are the ways people are supposed to
  act in groups.
People may have a different role in each
  group to which they belong.

Sometimes a person is a leader.
A leader's role is to help the group reach its
 goal.
Sometimes a person is a follower.
A follower's role is to listen to and help the
 leader.
A follower's role is also to help other
 followers.

CHECKING
MAIN
IDEAS

1. What are roles?
2. What roles do people have?

4 RULES WITHIN GROUPS

Different groups have different **rules.**
Rules tell us what to do and what not to do.
They help keep people safe.
Rules help people work and play together.

There are rules to follow at home.
One rule might be to keep your room clean.
There are rules to follow at school.
One rule might be to work quietly.

There are rules to follow in neighborhoods.
One rule might be to stay off the grass in
the park.

CHECKING
MAIN
IDEAS

1. What are rules?
2. What do rules help people do?

5 LOOKING AT PROBLEMS

Sometimes neighborhoods have problems.
There are many causes of problems in
 neighborhoods.

Problems can be caused by poor
  neighborhood planning.
Sometimes a neighborhood has more traffic
  than it can handle.
Some neighborhoods do not have enough
  places for children to play.

Problems can be caused when people do not
follow rules.
Sometimes people throw papers and garbage
on the street.
Sometimes factories give off thick smoke that
can harm people, plants, and other things.

Problems can be caused when people do not
take care of things they own.
Some buildings may need to be fixed.
Problems can make neighborhoods unsafe or
unclean.

CHECKING How are neighborhood problems caused?
MAIN
IDEAS

6 DOING SOMETHING ABOUT PROBLEMS

People work with their neighbors to solve
neighborhood problems.
Sometimes neighbors are worried about
neighborhood problems.

They get together to talk about the
  problems.
They decide what to do about the problems.
Then they do something about the problems.

Sometimes people work with community
leaders to solve problems.
The people in a neighborhood and the
community leaders talk about the
problems.
They decide what to do.

Then the community leaders help the people
in the neighborhood do something about
the problems.

CHECKING
MAIN
IDEAS

What steps do people take to solve
neighborhood problems?

Citizenship in Action

The Neighborhood Family

The Neighborhood Family is a group of
people who joined together in the 1970's
to solve neighborhood problems.

The members met every week to talk about
neighborhood problems.

They gave their ideas about what should be
done.

Then the members voted on the ideas.

In this way, all the members had a voice in
what the group did.

7 BEING A GOOD CITIZEN

People have many **rights.**

Rights are things that people should be allowed to do.

Rights should not be taken away from a person by anyone else.

Rules help protect people's rights.

People have a right to have a safe
neighborhood.
With this right goes the **responsibility** of
following rules.
A responsibility is a thing that people are
supposed to do.

People have a right to have a clean and
  enjoyable neighborhood.
With this right goes the responsibility of
  taking care of things.

CHECKING
MAIN
IDEAS

1. What are rights?
2. What is a responsibility?

8 GOING FORWARD TOGETHER

Neighbors plan what they want their
neighborhood to be like in the future.
Planning helps neighborhoods grow and
change in an orderly way.

Sometimes people do not agree about the
plans for their neighborhood.
They tell what they like and do not like
about the plans.
They suggest ways to change the plans.

Usually people can keep some of what they
 want.
Usually people have to give up some of what
 they want.

CHECKING MAIN IDEAS   What do people do if they do not agree
about neighborhood plans?

A Nation's Heritage

Benjamin Banneker

Benjamin Banneker worked as a **surveyor.**
A surveyor measures the size, the shape, and
the position of land.
A friend asked Benjamin to help plan
Washington, D.C.
Benjamin used special tools to do this work.
He helped plan where to build buildings.

INVESTIGATING THE UNIT

Write your answers on a separate sheet of paper.

Using Words and Terms

Use the following words or terms in a sentence to show that you understand their meaning:

roles   rights
rules   responsibility

Understanding Ideas

1. Why do people form groups?
2. What are some roles that people have?
3. How do rules help people?
4. How do people solve neighborhood problems?
5. What are some rights and some responsibilities that people have?

Building Your Skills

Use the bar graph to answer the questions that follow:

1. Which group do the most pupils belong to?

2. Which group do the fewest pupils belong to?

3. How many pupils belong to reading clubs?

4. Which group do six pupils belong to?

Make a bar graph to show the groups to which the pupils in your class belong.

Making Decisions

One rule the library in your neighborhood has is "No talking." Suppose you do not like this rule.

Do you still have the responsibility of keeping this rule? Why or why not?

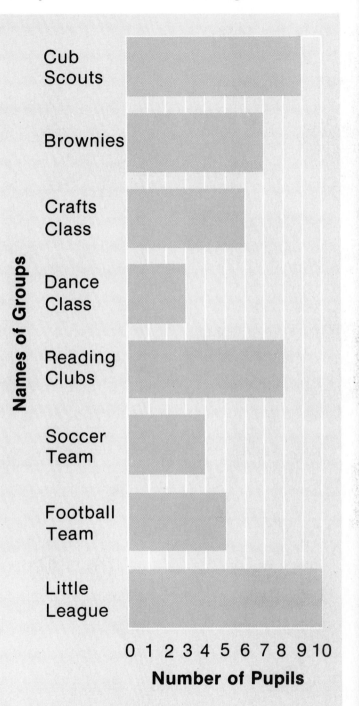

Groups to Which We Belong

Names of Groups: Cub Scouts, Brownies, Crafts Class, Dance Class, Reading Clubs, Soccer Team, Football Team, Little League

Number of Pupils: 0 1 2 3 4 5 6 7 8 9 10

UNIT 5
DIFFERENT KINDS OF
NEIGHBORHOODS

There are different kinds of neighborhoods.
Look at this picture.
What kinds of places does this neighborhood
     have?
How would you describe this neighborhood?

1 CITY NEIGHBORHOODS

City neighborhoods have many different
kinds of places to live.
Many people in a city live in apartment
buildings.
Other people live in houses.

Buildings in a city are usually close together.
So most city neighborhoods have few open
    spaces for children to play.
They also have little space for grass and
    trees.

Most city neighborhoods have some stores
and shops.
People in a neighborhood can fill some of
their needs and wants at these places.

Most city neighborhoods have **public transportation** so people can go to other places in the city.

Public transportation is a means of getting from one place to another.

It can be used by all the people of a community.

CHECKING MAIN IDEAS   What do most city neighborhoods have?

2 SUBURBAN NEIGHBORHOODS

Suburban neighborhoods are neighborhoods
near large cities.

These neighborhoods usually have newer
houses and apartments than city
neighborhoods have.

They have open spaces for play and for grass
and trees.

Suburban neighborhoods often have little
   public transportation.
People can usually take a train or a bus to
   the city.
Sometimes, however, they have to use their
   own car to get around in their
   community.

Suburban neighborhoods often have only a
few stores and shops at which to fill
needs and wants.
People living in these neighborhoods usually
go to shopping areas in their community.

These shopping areas are sometimes many
blocks from where most people live.
People living in suburban neighborhoods
also go to the city to fill their needs and
wants.

CHECKING What do suburban neighborhoods have?

MAIN

IDEAS

3 TOWN NEIGHBORHOODS

Town neighborhoods are usually many miles
   or kilometers from large cities.
Most of the people who live in town
   neighborhoods live in one-family houses.
However, some people live in apartments.

Town neighborhoods have little public
transportation.
People who live in these neighborhoods
usually use their car to go from place to
place.

Town neighborhoods have few stores and
shops.
These are usually located in the middle of
the town.
People go to these stores and shops or to a
city to fill their needs and wants.

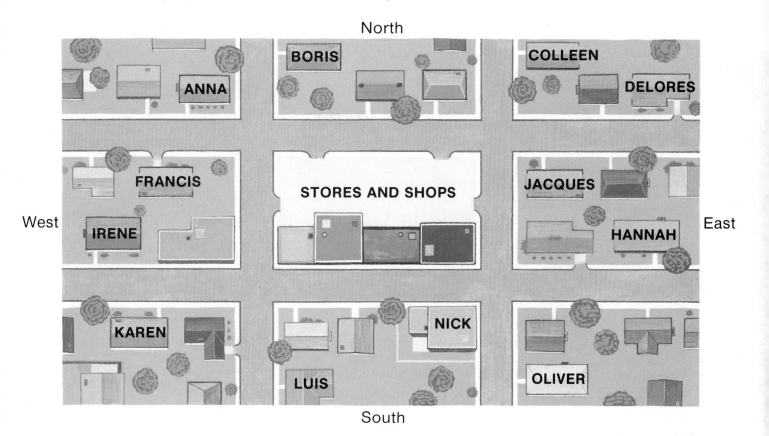

The map on this page shows part of a town.
Who lives closer to the stores and shops,
   Nick or Oliver?
What direction would Irene have to go to
   get to the stores and shops?

CHECKING What do town neighborhoods have?

MAIN

IDEAS

Citizenship in Action

Jerome, Arizona

Jerome is a town in Arizona.

Many years ago most of the people moved out of Jerome because the mine where they worked closed.

The people who stayed in Jerome fixed up their town.

They opened a mining museum and a gift shop.

Now Jerome is a nice place to live in and to visit.

4 FARM NEIGHBORHOODS

People who live in farm neighborhoods
usually live in one-family houses.
There are other farm buildings near their
house.
People live quite far apart from other people.
This is because the people living in farm
neighborhoods need a lot of land for their
farm.

Farm neighborhoods have no public
transportation.
People usually use their car or truck to go
from place to place.

Farm neighborhoods have no stores and
    shops.
People living in farm neighborhoods fill
    some of their needs and wants with what
    they raise on their farm.
They fill other needs and wants in a nearby
    town or city.

CHECKING
MAIN
IDEAS

How do people living in farm
neighborhoods fill their needs and wants?

5 CULTURAL NEIGHBORHOODS

Many people in cultural neighborhoods do
  special things.
They do these things because their family
  did them in the past.

The people sometimes speak another
language besides English.
They have dances, songs, and costumes to
help celebrate special days.
People in cultural neighborhoods sometimes
eat special foods.

Cultural neighborhoods are like other
   neighborhoods in many ways.
Cultural neighborhoods have places to live.
They have apartments and houses.
Cultural neighborhoods have places to shop.

130

Cultural neighborhoods have places of
learning and of worship.
They have places to have fun.

People in cultural neighborhoods belong to groups.

They follow rules.

They work together for the good of their neighborhood.

CHECKING MAIN IDEAS

1. What special things do people in cultural neighborhoods do?

2. How are cultural neighborhoods like other neighborhoods?

6 HISTORICAL NEIGHBORHOODS

A number of communities have **historical neighborhoods.**

These neighborhoods help us learn about people and places from the past.

They help us learn about things that happened in the past.

Many important things happened in the building shown on this page.

Historical neighborhoods might have special
    houses.
These houses show how people lived in the
    past.

Historical neighborhoods might have
monuments.
Some monuments are built where something
important happened.
Other monuments are built where important
buildings have been.

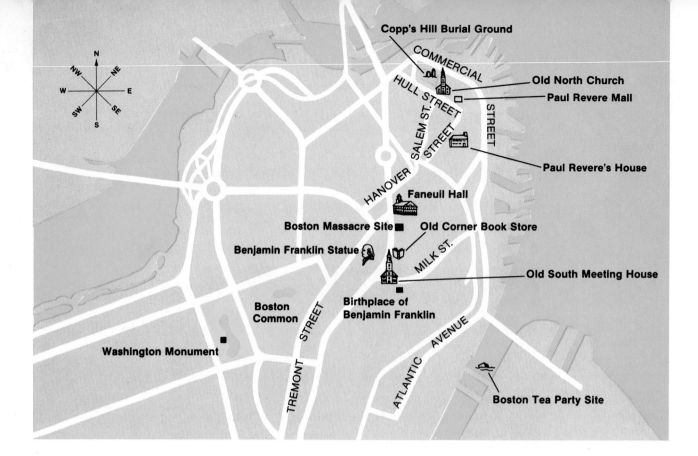

The map on this page is of part of a
historical neighborhood in Boston.
Find Paul Revere's House.
What direction is the Boston Tea Party Site
from Paul Revere's House?

CHECKING MAIN IDEAS

What do historical neighborhoods help us
learn about?

A Nation's Heritage

The Alamo

This is a picture of the Alamo.
The Alamo is in a historical neighborhood in
San Antonio, Texas.
Many years ago the Alamo was used as a
fort.
It was used by people from Texas who
fought against the Mexican Army.
The Alamo helps us remember how the
people of Texas fought for their freedom
from Mexico.

7 NEIGHBORHOODS CHANGE

Neighborhoods are always changing.
Time can cause neighborhoods to change.
Buildings get old and run-down.
They are torn down and new buildings are
    put in their place.

People can cause neighborhoods to change.
People move in and out of neighborhoods.
Sometimes people let their neighborhood
  become run-down.
Sometimes they help fix up their
  neighborhood.

Some changes are good for a neighborhood.
These changes help a neighborhood become
   better.
Some changes are not good.
These changes cause a neighborhood to
   become worse.
Changes that are not good should be
   stopped.

People can clean up and fix up a run-down
  neighborhood.
They can work to make their neighborhood
a place where people will want to live.

CHECKING MAIN IDEAS

1. How do neighborhoods change?
2. What causes neighborhoods to change?

INVESTIGATING
THE UNIT

Write your answers on a separate sheet of paper.

Using Words and Terms

Use the following words or terms in a sentence to show that you understand their meaning:

public transportation
historical neighborhoods

Understanding Ideas

1. What do most city neighborhoods have?

2. What do most suburban neighborhoods have?

3. What do most town neighborhoods have?

4. How do farmers fill their needs and wants?

5. What special things do people who live in cultural neighborhoods do?

6. What can we learn from historical neighborhoods?

7. Why do neighborhoods change?

Building Your Skills

Copy the chart to the right on a piece of paper. Place a ✓ next to the characteristics that each kind of neighborhood has.

Making Decisions

Of the neighborhoods studied, in which kind of neighborhood would you rather live?

Why did you choose that kind of neighborhood?

What might you like best about the kind of neighborhood you chose?

	City	Suburban	Farm
Houses			
Apartments			
Many Stores and Shops			
Few Stores and Shops			
Much Public Transportation			
Little Public Transportation			

UNIT 6
NEIGHBORHOODS THROUGHOUT THE WORLD

There are many neighborhoods throughout
   the world.
Some are like neighborhoods in the United
   States.
Some are different from neighborhoods in
   the United States.
Look at the picture on this page.
How is this neighborhood like your
   neighborhood?
How is it different?

1 LIVING IN ECUADOR

Rosa lives in the country of Ecuador
   [EK-wuh-DAWR].
She lives on a **hacienda** [AHS-ee-EN-duh]
   with her family.
A hacienda is a large farm.

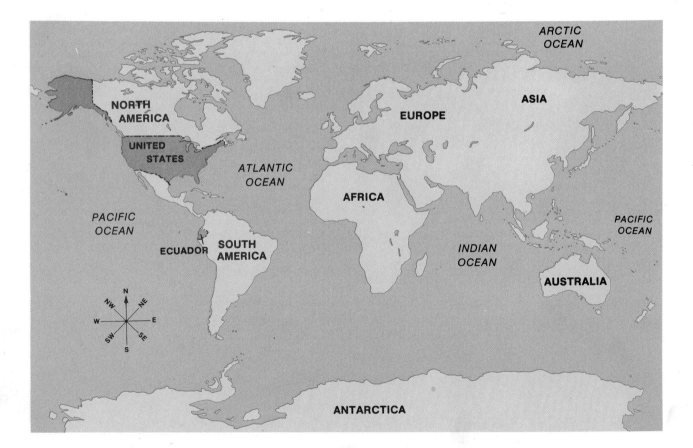

Many other families also live on the
  hacienda.
The families work for the owner of the
  hacienda.
They raise corn.
Rosa's family lives in a one-room house.
The roof of the house is made of grass.

Rosa's family has a garden.
Her family grows vegetables to help fill the
    family's need for food.
Rosa's family uses some of the corn to make
    bread and soup.

Rosa's family also raises a few sheep.
The wool from the sheep is used to make
cloth.
The cloth is used to make **ponchos**
[PAHN-chohz] and other clothes.
Ponchos are large pieces of cloth with an
opening in the middle for the head.

Rosa and her family go to an open-air
  market near their hacienda.
Here they sell the vegetables and the cloth
  they do not need.
They buy some food that they need.
They also buy **handicrafts**—things made by
  hand.

CHECKING
MAIN
IDEAS

How do Rosa and her family fill their
needs and wants?

2 LIVING IN ISRAEL

Ari [AR-ee] lives in the country of Israel
[IZ-ree-uhl].
Most of the people in Israel live in cities and
towns.

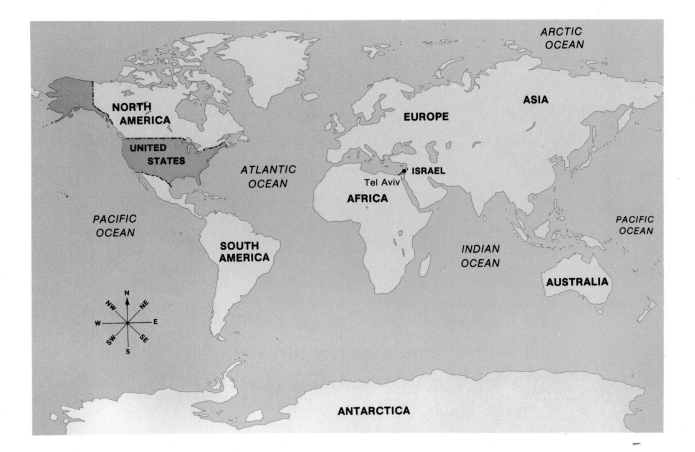

Ari lives in Tel Aviv [TEL-uh-VEEV].
Tel Aviv is the largest city in Israel.
Ari's neighborhood has many places that
    make goods.
Canned foods, clothes, and tools are some of
    the goods made there.

Many services like those provided in
neighborhoods in the United States are
also provided in Ari's neighborhood.
Teachers and doctors are among those who
provide services.

Like most of the people in Tel Aviv, Ari's
family lives in an apartment.
Ari's family can fill its needs and wants at
Dizengoff Circle.
Dizengoff Circle is a part of Tel Aviv that
has many stores and shops.

There are many schools and museums in Tel
Aviv for Ari's family to use.
Two important museums are the Museum
Haaretz and the Tel Aviv Museum.

There are also many places for Ari's family
to worship in Tel Aviv.
There are many places for Ari's family to
have fun—such as parks, theaters, and
Ramat Gan Stadium.

**CHECKING
MAIN
IDEAS**

What are some goods and services
provided in Ari's neighborhood?

Citizenship in Action

A Kibbutz in Israel

A person in Israel might live on a large farm
   called a **kibbutz** [kib-UTS].

It is owned by the people who live there.

The kibbutz helps the people fill their needs
   and wants.

The members of the kibbutz share the food
   they raise.

They also get their clothes from the kibbutz.

All the members of the kibbutz are expected
   to work on the kibbutz.

Some people work in the fields, and others
   perform services needed by the kibbutz.

3 LIVING IN KENYA

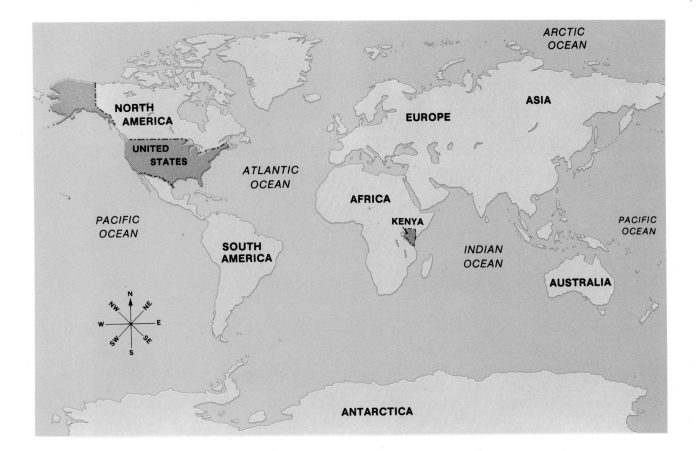

Kamau [kuh-MOW] is a boy who lives in the
country of Kenya [KEN-yuh].
He and his family live on a **homestead.**
A homestead is a farm and its buildings.

His family is part of a **clan.**
A clan is a group of related families.
The members of his clan get together to
celebrate special times.

Kamau's clan belongs to the Kikuyu
 [ki-KOO-yoo] **tribe.**
A tribe is a group made up of many clans.
The tribe protects the people from danger
 and helps the people do what is right.

Most of the boys and girls in Kamau's tribe
go to school.

When they are twelve years old, they may
become members of an age group.
Before they join the group, they must learn
about the tribe and how they should act.
The members of an age group are expected
to help the tribe.

160

There are many rules for Kamau to follow.
He must always speak to others in the
right way.
He must do what the older people in the
tribe tell him to do.
Kamau must take good care of the farm
animals.

CHECKING MAIN IDEAS

1. Which groups that Kamau belongs to are like the groups that you belong to? Which groups are different?

2. What rules must Kamau follow?

4 LIVING IN INDIA

Srinivas [SHREE-nee-vahs] is a boy who
    lives in the country of India [IN-dee-uh].
He lives in Calcutta [kal-KUHT-uh].
It is one of India's large cities.
Calcutta has a number of problems.
Many other cities around the world also
    have problems.

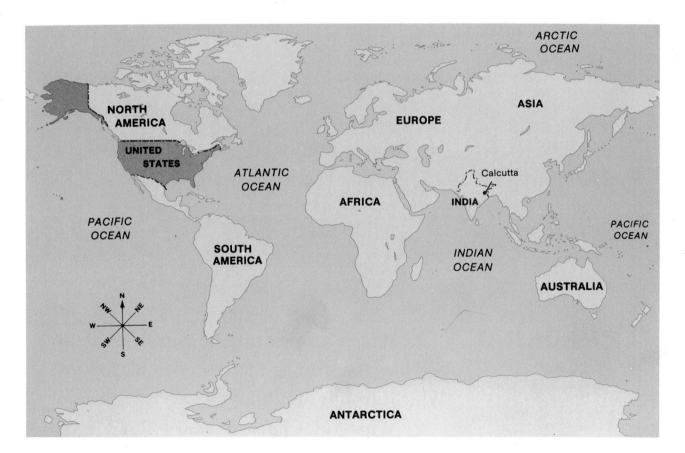

Like many cities in the world, Calcutta is
   not large enough for the number of
   people who live there.
The streets are usually crowded with traffic.
Srinivas lives in a nice house with his
   family.
Some people in Calcutta live in run-down
   houses.
Many people in Calcutta have to live
   crowded together in one house.
Many other people do not have a place to
   live.

Few of the houses in Calcutta have running
water.
Srinivas and his family get their water from
an open well.
Often the water is not good.
Sometimes it causes people to get sick.

Many people in Calcutta are poor.
They have little money to buy the food they
    need.
Srinivas goes to school.
However, some children in India cannot go
    to school because they are needed to
    work.

Some problems in Calcutta and in other
cities in India are being solved.
People can borrow money to build better
houses.
Better medicines and new hospitals are
helping people who are sick.
Special schools are helping to train people
for jobs so that they can have a better
life.

CHECKING MAIN IDEAS

1. What are some problems Calcutta has?
2. How are some of the problems in Calcutta being solved?

5 LIVING IN DENMARK

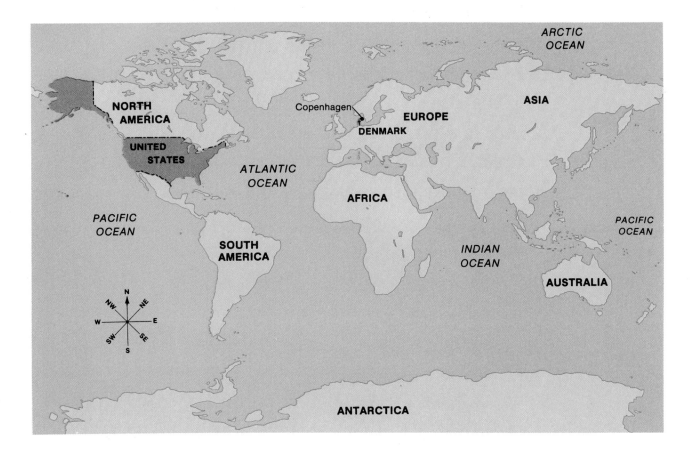

Helge [HEL-guh] lives in the country of
Denmark [DEN-MAHRK].
She lives in the city of Copenhagen
[KOH-puhn-HAY-guhn].
Copenhagen is the largest city in Denmark.

Helge and her family live in an apartment.
Nearly all the people in Copenhagen live in apartments.
Helge's family goes to the "walking street," which has many stores and shops, to fill some of the family's needs and wants.
Her family uses a bus or a **tram** to go places in the city.
A tram is a car that runs on rails in the street.
Helge's family also uses a car and a bicycle.

There are many small towns in Denmark.
Most of the people in towns live in
   one-family houses.
They usually use their bicycle to go from
   place to place.
However, sometimes they use their car.
The people in a town go to the small shops
   in the town to fill some of their needs
   and wants.

Some people in Denmark live on farms.
They live in one-family houses.
Near the house there is usually a barn and
   other farm buildings.

Farmers build these buildings in a square,
   with a large open place in the middle.
Most farms also have a pond for ducks.

Farmers in Denmark work together to sell
part of what they raise.
The farmers also use some of the pigs, the
chickens, and the cows that they raise to
fill some of their needs and wants.
They go to a nearby town to fill other needs
and wants.

CHECKING MAIN IDEAS

1. How is Helge's neighborhood like urban neighborhoods in the United States? How is it different?

2. How are rural neighborhoods in Denmark like rural neighborhoods in the United States? How are they different?

Practicing Your Skills

Reading a Map

This map shows the Tivoli Gardens
    amusement park in Copenhagen,
    Denmark.
Use the map to answer these questions.
What is the first thing north of the car ride?
What direction is the pond from the boat
    ride?
What is the first thing east of the train ride?
What does the symbol ☺ stand for?

Key

🏛 Main Entrance
🚗 Car Ride
☺ Fun House
⛵ Boat Ride
⬭ Pond
🎆 Ferris Wheel
🚂 Train Ride
🎠 Merry-go-round

6 LIVING IN SOUTH KOREA

Sumi [SOO-mee] lives in the country of
South Korea [kuh-REE-uh].
This country is also called the Republic of
Korea.

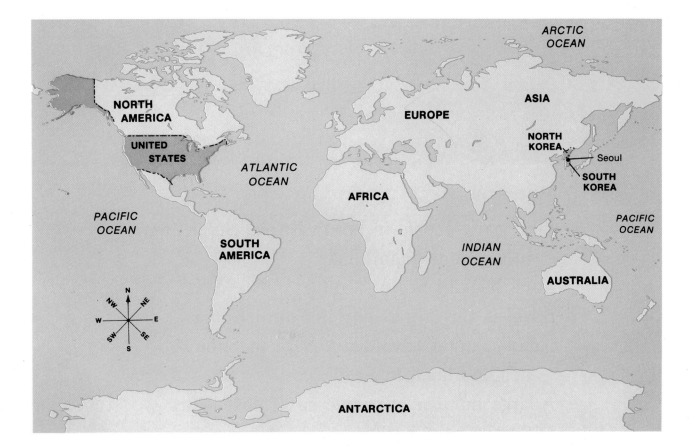

Like many people in South Korea, Sumi lives
    in a city neighborhood.
Sumi lives in Seoul [SOHL].
Seoul is the largest city in South Korea.
Many changes have taken place in Sumi's
    neighborhood in Seoul.
A large number of people have moved into
    Sumi's neighborhood.
So more places to live have been built.

There is more traffic in Seoul than there
used to be.
So the streets have been widened.
Sumi's family uses the new **subway** that has
been built to make it easier for people to
get around in the city.
A subway is an electric train that runs under
the ground.

175

Changes have also taken place in farm
   neighborhoods.
In the past, summer rains often flooded the
   rice fields.
These floods would wash away the seeds.
Now the farmers have built **dikes.**
Dikes are walls used to hold water back.

In the past, most of the people of South
  Korea were farmers.
Now many of the farmers have gone to work
  in factories.
These factories make goods, most of which
  are shipped to other countries.

CHECKING   What changes have taken place in South

MAIN   Korea?

IDEAS

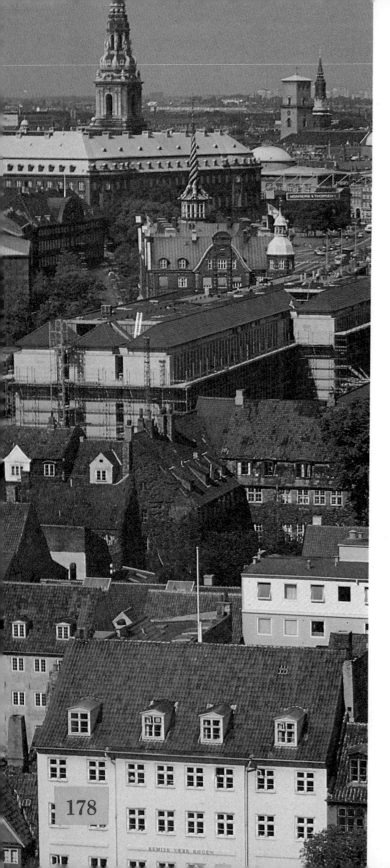

INVESTIGATING THE UNIT

Write your answers on a separate sheet of paper.

Using Words and Terms

Use the following words or terms in a sentence to show that you understand their meaning:

hacienda	tribe
clan	kibbutz

Understanding Ideas

1. How does Rosa's family fill its needs and wants?
2. What goods are provided in Ari's neighborhood?
3. What groups does Kamau belong to?
4. How are problems in Calcutta being solved?

5. How is Helge's neighborhood like urban neighborhoods in the United States? How is it different?

6. What are some changes that have taken place in South Korea?

Building Your Skills

Write the numbers 1 to 4 on your paper. Write the letter of the word that goes with each picture.

  a. homestead
  b. tribe
  c. dike
  d. tram
  e. poncho

Making Decisions

Which of the neighborhoods you have studied would you like to visit? Why did you choose the neighborhood you chose?

Handbook

180

The United States

Key

~~~~~ River

● Largest City

★ Capital of the United States

The World

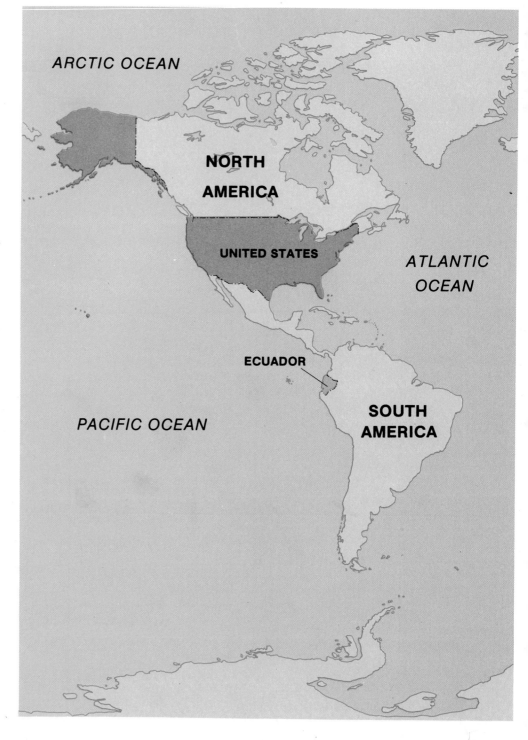

ARCTIC OCEAN

NORTH
AMERICA

UNITED STATES

ATLANTIC
OCEAN

ECUADOR

PACIFIC OCEAN

SOUTH
AMERICA

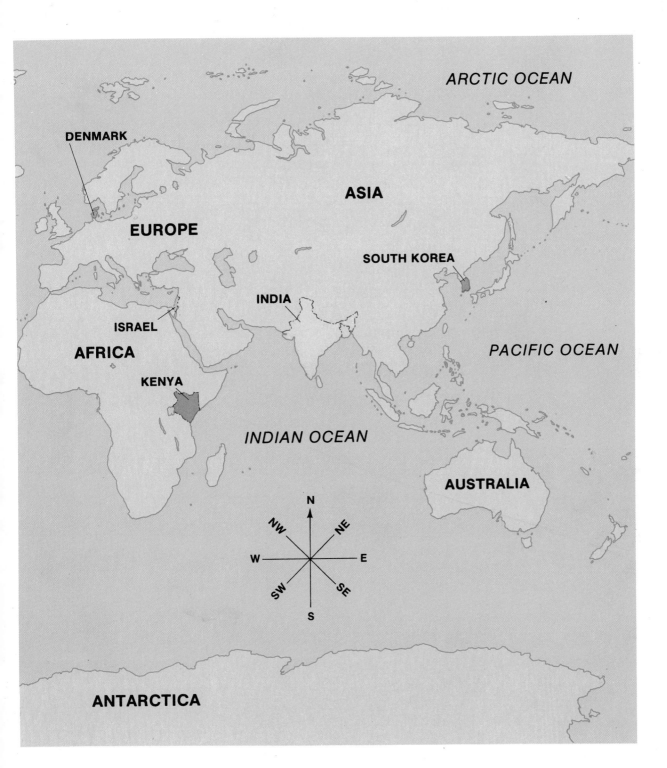

Information About Selected Countries of the World

Country	Land Size	Number of People	Capital
United States	3,618,467 sq mi 9 371 829 sq km	230,860,000	Washington, D.C.
Ecuador	109,484 sq mi 283 561 sq km	8,930,000	Quito
Israel	7,993 sq mi 20 700 sq km	4,116,000	Jerusalem
Kenya	224,960 sq mi 582 646 sq km	16,840,000	Nairobi
India	1,222,712 sq mi 3 166 828 sq km	692,860,000	New Delhi
Denmark	16,631 sq mi 43 075 sq km	5,180,000	Copenhagen
South Korea	38,031 sq mi 98 500 sq km	39,556,000	Seoul

Largest City	Major Goods	Official Languages	National Song
New York	Beef cattle, milk, corn, soy beans, metal products	English	"The Star-Spangled Banner"
Guayaquil	Bananas, grains, cacao, balsa wood, cement, chemicals, textiles	Spanish	"Himno Nacional del Ecuador" ("National Anthem of Ecuador")
Jerusalem	Citrus fruits, textiles, finished diamonds, salts, machinery, chemicals	Hebrew Arabic	"Hatikva" ("The Hope")
Nairobi	Coffee, corn, tea, meat, sisal, light machinery	Swahili	"Wimbo wa Taifa" ("Anthem of the Nation")
Bombay	Cotton, jute, rice, tea, sugar cane, wheat, steel, fertilizer, bauxite, mica	Hindi	"Jana-gana-mana" ("Thou Art the Ruler of the Minds of All People")
Copenhagen	Barley, beef and dairy cattle, potatoes, grains, machinery, ships	Danish	"Der er et yndigt land" ("There Is a Lovely Land")
Seoul	Beans, rice, wheat, iron ore, chemicals, graphite, tungsten, shellfish	Korean	"Aegug-ka" ("National Anthem")*

* Used as the unofficial national song

BOOKS TO READ

GLOSSARY

alphabetical order

Children in Neighborhoods

Neighborhood	Number of Children
Bob's	7
Sue's	9

chart

apartment

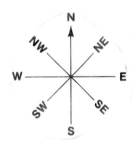

compass rose

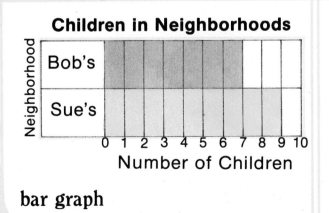

bar graph

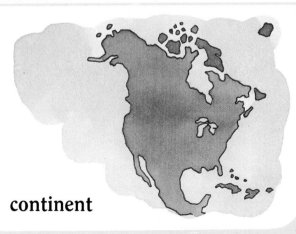

continent

187

dike

goods

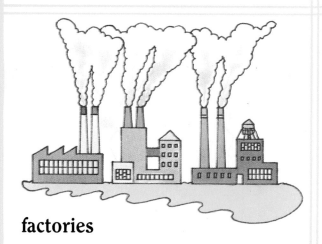

factories

handicrafts

globe

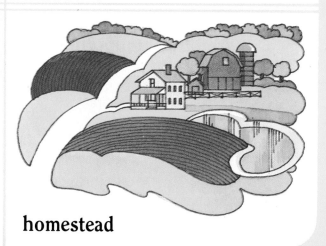

homestead

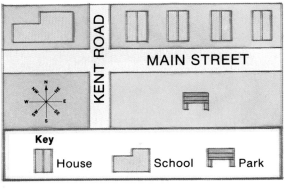

map

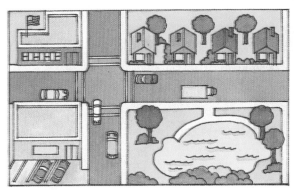

neighborhood

mobile homes

neighbors

needs

oceans

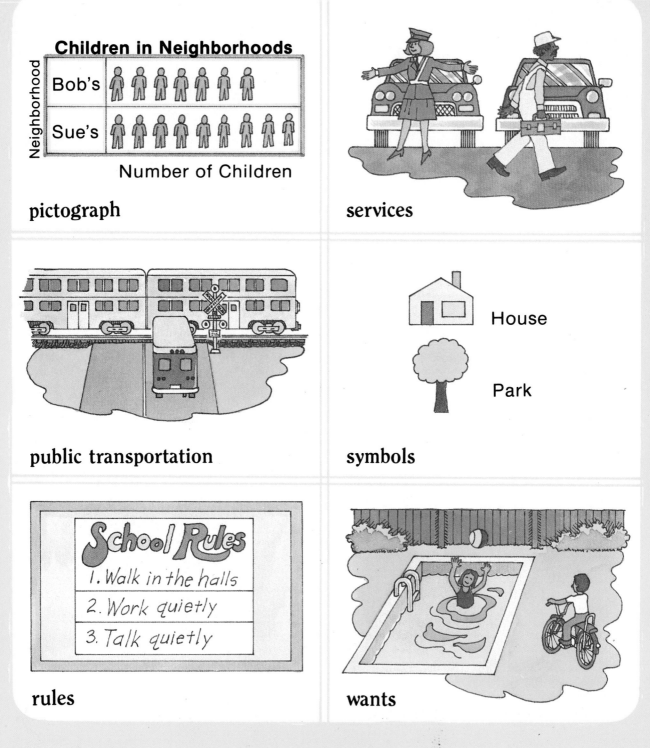

Children in Neighborhoods

Neighborhood	Number of Children
Bob's	🧍🧍🧍🧍🧍🧍
Sue's	🧍🧍🧍🧍🧍🧍🧍🧍🧍

Number of Children

pictograph

services

public transportation

House

Park

symbols

School Rules
1. Walk in the halls
2. Work quietly
3. Talk quietly

rules

wants

INDEX